Anne Frank

Copyright © 2018 by Quelle Histoire / quellehistoire.com
Published by Roaring Brook Press
Roaring Brook Press is a division of Holtzbrinck Publishing Holdings Limited Partnership
175 Fifth Avenue, New York, NY 10010
mackids.com

Library of Congress Control Number: 2018936547
ISBN 978-1-250-16877-1

Our books may be purchased in bulk for promotional, educational, or business use. Please contact your local bookseller or the Macmillan Corporate and Premium Sales Department at (800) 221-7945 ext. 5442 or by e-mail at MacmillanSpecialMarkets@macmillan.com.

First published in France in 2017 by Quelle Histoire, Paris
First U.S. edition, 2018

Text: Clémentine V. Baron
Translation: Catherine Nolan
Illustrations: Bruno Wennagel, Mathieu Ferret, Aurélie Verdon, Guillaume Biasse, Aurélien Fernandez, Mathilde Tuffin, Nuno Alves Rodrigues

Printed in China by RR Donnelley Asia Printing Solutions Ltd., Dongguan City, Guangdong Province
10 9 8 7 6 5 4 3 2 1

Anne Frank

Roaring Brook Press
New York

First Years

Annelies Marie Frank was born in Germany in 1929. Everyone called her Anne.

The first years of Anne's life were happy. She lived with her parents, Otto and Edith, and her older sister, Margot. The two sisters were opposites. Margot was calm and serious. Anne could not sit still!

That didn't stop them from having many friends in common. Some of their friends were Jewish, like them. Others were Catholic or Protestant.

The Frank girls and their friends did not care that they came from different religions. But across Germany, a wave of hatred against Jews was starting to spread.

———

1929–1933

Hitler Rises to Power

One of the people spreading the hate was a politician named Adolf Hitler. Hitler made horrible speeches about Jews, accusing them of being evil.

In 1933, Hitler was appointed chancellor of Germany and soon gained control of the country. Life grew very hard for Jews there. Anne's family decided to leave. They packed up their bags and headed to the Netherlands.

———

1933

A New Life in Amsterdam

The Franks settled in the city of Amsterdam. For a while, they were safe. They lived normal lives. Anne's father started a company that sold ingredients for jam. Anne and Margot went to school.

Then Hitler's army invaded the country of Poland, and World War II broke out. Soon his army invaded the Netherlands, too. Everything changed for the Franks and for all the Jews in Amsterdam.

—————

1933–1940

The Fall

Now Anne and Margot had to go to a special school. They had to wear yellow stars on their chests to show that they were Jews.

One day in 1942, Margot got a letter. She was supposed to report to a labor camp.

Labor camps were awful places. People who went there were forced to work until they collapsed. Many of them died.

The Franks made a decision: They wouldn't let Margot report to the camp. Instead, the family would go into hiding.

———

1940–1942

Life in Hiding

Anne's father knew a place to hide. His business had a secret annex—an area with a few small rooms—attached to its offices. The entrance was hidden by a bookcase. The Frank family went there. Soon, four more people joined them.

Otto's assistant, Miep Gies, and her husband, Jan, brought food and news from the outside world. Three other friends helped, too. Everyone thought this was a temporary solution. The Franks figured they would hide for a few months. They didn't know they would live in the annex for two years!

———

1942–1944

Anne's Diary

Shhhhh! The family learned to live in silence. There was no talking, running, or even flushing the toilet during the day.

Anne spent her time writing. Just before going into hiding, she received a notebook for her birthday. It was covered in red-and-white plaid cloth, and it closed with a small clasp in the front. Anne turned the notebook into a diary. She described life in the annex. "We're as still as baby mice," she wrote. "I'm terrified our hiding place will be discovered."

_____

1942–1944

The Annex

Months passed. The war raged on. Countries banded together to fight Hitler's army. Their planes flew over the Netherlands, on the way to drop bombs on Germany.

One evening, Anne heard on the radio how important it was to write down stories about the war. She realized her little diary could be a valuable piece of history. Anne started rewriting her diary, including more details. She hoped someday she could turn her story into a book called *The Annex*.

———

1944

Discovered

In August 1944, Anne's worst fear came true: Her family was discovered. The police came and arrested them. What happened? Did someone turn them in? The world will never know.

After the Franks were taken away, Miep went into the annex. She spotted Anne's diary on the floor. She picked it up and carefully hid it away in her desk. *When the war is over and Anne returns, I will give it back to her*, she thought to herself.

She did not know that Anne would never come back.

———

1944

Otto's Return

The Franks were sent to concentration camps—brutal places where Jews and other Nazi victims were imprisoned and killed. Otto was separated from Edith, Anne, and Margot.

Otto survived the camp. After the war, he began the long journey home. Along the way, he found out that Edith had died. He had no news of his daughters. He searched and searched for them, and at last he learned the terrible truth: Both girls had died of typhus, a deadly disease that had spread through the camp.

Otto was devastated.

———

1945

A Famous Writer

Otto was still in shock when Miep gave him Anne's diary.

Otto began to read. He was astonished. Anne's writing was beautiful. It was hard to believe that such powerful words were written by a fourteen-year-old.

Otto remembered that Anne had wanted to publish a book after the war. He decided to respect her wish. *Anne Frank: The Diary of a Young Girl* was published in 1947. Readers everywhere were moved by Anne's story.

Today, the book is taught in schools around the world. Imagine if Anne Frank had known that she would become one of the most famous and admired writers of all time!

———

1947

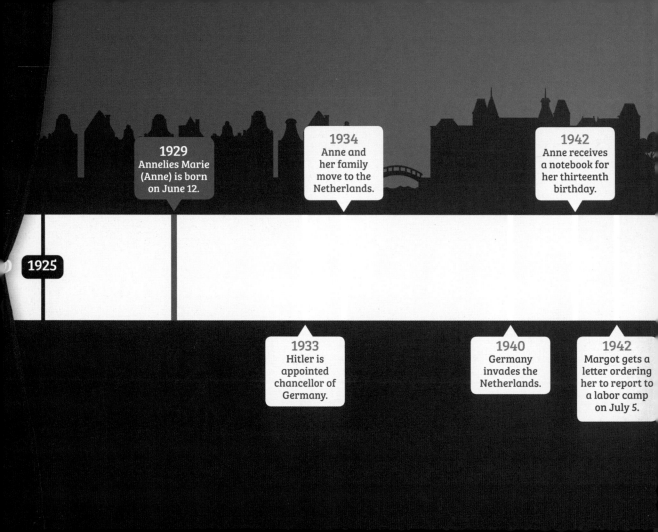

1929
Annelies Marie (Anne) is born on June 12.

1934
Anne and her family move to the Netherlands.

1942
Anne receives a notebook for her thirteenth birthday.

1925

1933
Hitler is appointed chancellor of Germany.

1940
Germany invades the Netherlands.

1942
Margot gets a letter ordering her to report to a labor camp on July 5.

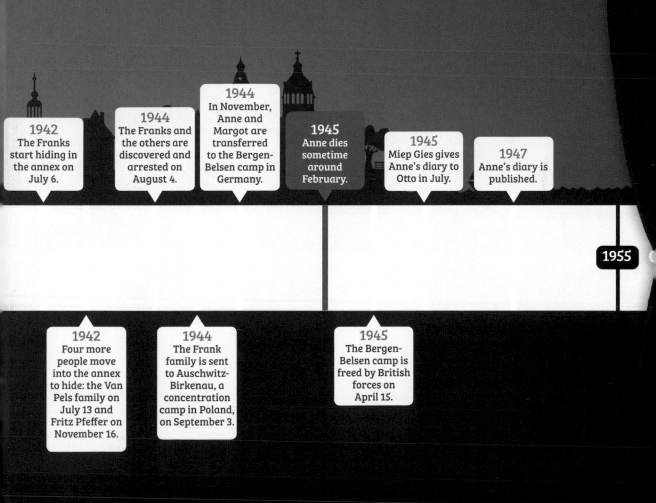

1942
The Franks start hiding in the annex on July 6.

1944
The Franks and the others are discovered and arrested on August 4.

1944
In November, Anne and Margot are transferred to the Bergen-Belsen camp in Germany.

1945
Anne dies sometime around February.

1945
Miep Gies gives Anne's diary to Otto in July.

1947
Anne's diary is published.

1955

1942
Four more people move into the annex to hide: the Van Pels family on July 13 and Fritz Pfeffer on November 16.

1944
The Frank family is sent to Auschwitz-Birkenau, a concentration camp in Poland, on September 3.

1945
The Bergen-Belsen camp is freed by British forces on April 15.

Anne Frank's Journey

1 Frankfurt am Main, Germany

Anne and Margot were born in this German city. The Franks lived a peaceful life in Frankfurt.

 2 Amsterdam, the Netherlands

After Hitler was appointed chancellor in 1933, the Frank family moved to the Netherlands, settling in Amsterdam. They were safe there until 1940, when Hitler's army invaded the country.

 3 Annex, the Netherlands

The Franks hid in an annex at Otto's workplace for two years. The annex was just a few rooms, located behind the offices, with an entrance concealed by a bookcase.

 4 Westerbork, the Netherlands

After their arrest, the Franks were taken to the Westerbork transit camp. During the days they worked, but in the evenings they were allowed to sit and talk. They hoped they wouldn't be sent to concentration camps, which they knew were far worse.

 5 Auschwitz-Birkenau, Poland

On September 3, 1944, the family boarded a train to a concentration camp in Poland called Auschwitz. The journey lasted three days. At the camp, the prisoners were sorted—women on one side of the camp, men on the other. Otto never saw his wife and daughters again.

6 Bergen-Belsen, Germany

The Nazis, worried about approaching enemy troops, moved their prisoners to Germany. In November 1944, Anne and Margot were sent to the Bergen-Belsen concentration camp. Because of overcrowding and filthy living conditions, diseases spread in the camp.

People to Know

Otto Frank
(1889–1980)
Anne's father, Otto, fought for Germany during the First World War. He even received a medal. But his heroic past did not help him once the German government turned against Jews.

Margot Frank
(1926–1945)
Anne's older sister, Margot, was well-behaved, shy, religious, and passionate about math. She stayed by Anne's side when Anne caught typhus in the concentration camp and then fell ill herself.

Miep Gies
(1909–2010)

Miep was Otto's office assistant and a close
friend of the family. When the Franks went into
hiding, she helped them. She found and kept
Anne's diary after the Franks' arrest.

Adolf Hitler
(1889–1945)

Hitler was named chancellor of Germany in
1933. He spread hatred against Jews. His rule
led to the deadliest conflict in history.

....

Anne was a huge fan of Hollywood movies. She decorated her walls in the secret annex with pictures of movie stars.

....

In school, Anne was known as the class clown. Her math teacher called her "Mistress Chatterback" because she talked so much in class!

....

Anne dreamed of becoming a famous author when she grew up. Not only did she write in her diary, but she also wrote short stories and essays during her time in hiding.

....

Anne's sister, Margot, wrote a diary, too, but it was never found.

Available Now

Muhammad Ali

Neil Armstrong

Blackbeard

Coco Chanel

Charlie Chaplin

Cleopatra

Marie Curie

Albert Einstein

Anne Frank

Gandhi

Frida Kahlo

Martin Luther King Jr.

Abraham Lincoln

Nelson Mandela

Isaac Newton

Rosa Parks

Coming Soon

Marie Antoinette

Buddha

Pocahontas

Vincent van Gogh